Make a Worm Farm

words by Jill McDougall
photographs by Russell Millard

You will need:

a big plastic bottle
⇩

⇧
a cup of soil

half a cup of sand
⇩

⇧
a water spray

a bit of apple
⇩

⇧
some leaves

⇧
4 or 5 worms

1. Cut the top off the bottle.

2. Put some soil in the bottle.

3. Spray the soil with water.

Do not make it too wet.

4. Put some sand in the bottle.

5. Spray the sand with water.

6. Put more soil on top.

7. Spray the soil with water.

8. Cut up some apple.

9. Put the apple on the soil.

10. Put some leaves on the apple.

11. Put in the worms.

It is a worm farm.